D0519751

The Quest

Written and illustrated
by Seb Burnett

Waterford City and County
Libraries

OXFORD
UNIVERSITY PRESS

WATERFORD CITY AND COUNTY
WITHDRAWN
LIBRARY

The Adventure Crew

Dramalina the Elf

Dramalina is a proud and noble elf-maiden. She is the leader of the Adventure Crew and can be quite bossy. She LOVES adventure but doesn't like pickles.

Fakebeard the Great

Fakebeard is a shrewd and powerful wizard known throughout the land as a great magician. And definitely not a lady.

WITHDRAWN
WAKEFIELD CITY AND COUNTY LIBRARIES

Brian the Barbarian

Brian, son of Gondorr, is the strongest man in the land. He actually prefers reading to wrestling, and dreams of becoming a librarian barbarian one day.

Grimblegroo the Dwarf

Grimblegroo isn't really partial to adventure but he does like treasure, so he goes along with the others in case they find any.

It started like any other day in the Adventure Crew's crumbly cottage ...
Sigh! I'm so BORED!
Uh-oh! Dramalina is in one of her moods again ...
We haven't had an adventure for ages.
SPLAT!
Not since that disaster when we squashed Princess Pumpkin with a Mud troll.

Yes, she was pretty mad after that!
It's not funny, guys. The treasure chest is almost empty. Soon there won't be any money for biscuits.
She was furious – hopping mud, you could say!
Sigh. Maybe we aren't cut out to be adventurers ...
I mean, Brian, you like browsing books more than bashing goblins.
It says here that most bands of adventurers split up after two years.
ADVENTURE THE FACTS
Hocus-pocus, vac-there, vac-here – dirt and crumbs now ... DISAPPEAR!
Fakebeard, there is something weird about your wizardry.

And Grimblegroo, you are the laziest person I have ever met!
Shhh! I'm trying to watch You've Been Maimed.
Aaaaarrrghgh!
That's it! I GIVE UP!
Uh-oh! Mad elf alert!
Just then ...
RING RING
The Adventure Phone!

Hello. Adventure Crew at your service! No adventure too big or too small. How can we help you?
Oh ... yes ... uh-huh ... uh-huh ... yes ... OK.
Is Prince Percy stuck up a tree again?
No. It was my mum. She wants us to get her some milk from ...
Who was that on the phone?
THE GOBLIN KING'S SUPERMARKET!
An adventure at last! A quest for the juice of the noble cow.
Oooh! I'll change my shoes.
Oh. Great. That's miles away.

Nearly 3 hours later ...
OK. I think I've got everything.
At last!
The map says we have to go this way – through the Forest of Pain.
Off we go!
Are you absolutely sure this is the right way?
Yes, of course I'm –
WAAAAAAAA!

Aaarrrggghhh!
OOOFFF!
SPLAT!
Dramalina! Are you all right?
Yes. Yes, I'm fine.
OW! How embarrassing!
At least now we know why it's called the Forest of Pain.

Errr ... does anyone else get the feeling that we're being watched?
Oh dear. Really? Does my head look big in this hat?
Come on, everybody. According to the map, the supermarket is this way.
Ah! It's so nice to be back on an adventure.
I think we're going to get a lot more *adventure* any minute now ...

I'm really enjoying spending some quality time with you guys.
And it's lovely to be out in the fresh air, isn't it?
We should definitely do this more often.
Take that!
Oh, but the map says to be careful of wood gremlins around here. Packs of them sometimes jump out and attack travellers.
Ow! Get off!
So keep your eyes open!
Phew! I think we've scared them off.
Hey! Are you guys listening to me?
Wood gremlins!
Exactly! We should be extra vigilant – you never know what might happen!

Hmmmm. Uh-oh ...
Looks like we may have gone the wrong way. But it's OK. We can take a short cut through ...
THE SWAMP OF UNBEARABLE STINKINESS!
And this must be it.
Eurgghh! My nose!
The swamp is seriously stinky! To give you an idea of just how ghastly it smells, try to imagine your dad's socks stuffed with mouldy cheese and sat on by a skunk. Well ... it's ten times WORSE than that!

Fakebeard, have you got any magic spells that can help?
Let me see. I must have something in my magic bag.
I don't feel very well.
This is even worse than your socks, Brian.
Aha! This should do the trick!
TA-DA!
Clothes pegs?!
The smell has disappeared! MAGIC!
This is definitely not magic, Fakebeard.

With their magic clothes pegs stopping the dreadful smell, our band of brave adventurers soon reach the other side of the swamp.
We're nearly at the supermarket.
My nose hurts and I want a biscuit.
It's just at the top of ...
The Monstrous Mountains of Menace!

Come on, guys. Let's go! If we start climbing now, we should get there by Tuesday!
WAIT!
I've got a better idea – why don't we just take an eagle to the top?
BEEP BEEP BEEP
Screeeech! Where to, mate?
SWOOSH
The top of Mount Menace, please!
My beard's going to get in a terrible mess!
This is cheating.

Aargh!
Ouch!
Oi! Call that a safe landing?
SPLAT!
Well, the landing was an adventure.
I think I've broken my helmet!
Shhhhh! We have to be extremely quiet!
There it is! The Goblin King's Supermarket!
And it's being guarded by ogres!

Sigh! We'll never get past those ogres.
They're gigantic!
We will! We just need to think of a cunning and ingenious plan.
Hmm. Come on, Brian! Think ... Think ... Think ... Think ... Think ...
Finally, Brian comes up with a plan ...
I've got it! First, we need to build a large trebuchet, which is a catapult that will send us zooming over the supermarket walls. Then, Grimblegroo can distract the ogres by ...
Huh? Where did everyone go?
Brian! Over here!
Who said that?
It's me! Put on your cloak of invisibility!

Quietly sneaking past the guards ...
CHAIN MAIL SALE
50% OFF
Bruce, did four invisible adventurers just sneak past us?
GRRR
I don't know, Bob. I was reading this comic.
... our brave explorers find themselves inside the supermarket at last.
It's enormous! How will we find the milk?
My trebuchet would have worked too, you know.
Be careful now. The Goblin King is really devious and this place is like a maze. We MUST stick together.
YUM
BISCUITS
Mmmmm ... biscuits.

Grimblegroo wanders off in search of a snack.
Mmmm. Yummy biscuits!
CRISPS
CRISPS
CRISPS
But these were no ordinary biscuits. These were enchanted monster biscuits!
Choc chip! My favourite!
Uh-oh!
Prepare to face my fury!
Where's Grimblegroo?
We're almost there. We just need to get through the freezer section.
SPECIAL OFFER!
GET FREE!
Look out for polar bears and penguins!

It's very quiet ... almost TOO quiet.
Ah – look! Something cute is trying to talk to us. What's that, little buddy?
No! Don't open the freezer!
Oops!
Arghh! Flying fish fingers!
Brian! Help us!
Wait! I've got to read this book.
Briii-aaan!
This is no time for reading!
Hmmm. Left over right, through the loop and pull.
KNOTS
Knowledge is power!

Finally, our heroes arrive at the milk cabinet.
Yay! We did it! Now let's get Mum's milk and get out of here!
Look – I found a trolley.
So! You think you have defeated the Goblin King? Did you honestly think I'd let you buy milk that easily? Guards! Seize them!
Goblins!
Quick! Into the trolley!
Hurry Brian! They're gaining on us!
Ummm ... how do you steer this thing?
Arrrgggghhhhh!

You will never escape the Goblin King's Supermarket!
Quick! There's the check-out!
We will put you in jars and stack you with the pickles!
Nooooo!
Look! It's Grimblegroo!
How dare you eat me?
Argghh! Cardboard boxes!
Grab him, Brian!
CRASH!
Hey, guys! Am I glad to see you again!
Would you like a bag?
No, thank you! Keep the change!

KA-BOOM!
Let's go home!
Thank you for shopping at the Goblin King's Supermarket!
I wonder why I don't get many customers?
Dramalina, here's a note from your mum ... she says she forgot to ask you to pick up some sugar, so could you go back?
Noooooooooooo!

About the author

Hello. I'm Seb. I grew up in Lincolnshire but now live in Bristol with my wife and daughter. I work as an illustrator and animator so I get to make up stories and draw monsters every day. I also like biscuits.

The Quest is a true story, actually. I live next door to Dramalina's mum and she told me all about it.